Element
Rachel McCarthy

Rachel McCarthy

Enjoy!

Edinburgh 2015

smith|doorstop

Published 2015 by
smith|doorstop Books
The Poetry Business
Bank Street Arts
32-40 Bank Street
Sheffield S1 2DS

ISBN 978-1-910367-45-2
Typeset by Utter
Printed by MPG Biddles

Acknowledgements

My thanks to: *BBC Radio 4, BBC Radio Devon, Sky Arts, Antony Gormley and his 'One & Other' Project* and *Shearsman Books,* who aired/published some of the following poems in their early forms. My thanks too to Pan Macmillan and *The Bookseller* for publishing my essays and critiques written during the period in which *Element* was developed.

Heartfelt thanks to those who have provided encouragement and advice, in particular: Fiona Benson, Piran Bishop, Fiona Carroll, Carrie Etter, the volunteers at ExCite Poetry, Tony Frazer, Harry Guest, Katie Moudry, Ruth Padel, the Mincing Poets, Lawrence Sail and, last but not least, to Carol Ann Duffy. A further thank you to the Met Office, for granting me unpaid leave to finish the pamphlet. Finally my thanks to my family for their love and forbearance.

smith|doorstop Books are a member of Inpress:
www.inpressbooks.co.uk. Distributed by Central Books Ltd.,
99 Wallis Road, London E9 5LN

The Poetry Business gratefully acknowledges the support
of Arts Council England.

Supported by
**ARTS COUNCIL
ENGLAND**

Contents

Poets say science takes away from the beauty of the stars – mere globs of gas atoms. I too can see the stars on a desert night, and feel them. But do I see less or more? The vastness of the heavens stretches my imagination – stuck on this carousel my little eye can catch one – million – year-old light. A vast pattern – of which I am a part ... What is the pattern, or the meaning, or the why? It does not do harm to the mystery to know a little about it. For far more marvelous is the truth than any artists of the past imagined it. Why do the poets of the present not speak of it? What men are poets who can speak of Jupiter if he were a man, but if he is an immense spinning sphere of methane and ammonia must be silent?

– Richard P. Feynman

Each of the following poems take their starting point from the transition metal elements known to science by 1869, the year Dmitri Mendeleev published his periodic table.

Early Sun

Regarding your countless incarnations:
Helios the flame-haired charioteer
Ram-headed Ra on his funeral barge
Sól the divine seer flustered by fear,
each day you're some form of Dawn
Eos pouring out a tall jug of tears
in her dressing gown of jewel-bright saffron.

What to make then of this crocus
reed-steady in the morning's flow –
not her unwavering focus
on her fine filaments of gold
but her chrysalid argument
to hold on to our sadnesses –
who's made of herself a thimble of dew.

On Seeing Two Followers of Cadmus Devoured by a Dragon

(Cornelius van Haarlem)

Stand far enough away and the bite's a kiss,
his hand on its neck an embrace.
Either way the moment's about relenting.

How then to be sorry for their flesh?
Never stronger or as vulnerable as this –
splayed but bone steady, clinched

and into our cool space they lean, ardent,
uncurl like a fern's tongue
a pined-for garden, you and I

sudden and inchoate, horizoned:
the vanishing point where we should start,
the tip of the spear aimed at the heart.

Memorial at Norilsk

We're close
the pines thinning out and our road a slew
steering us into the wide, blank stare of the Steppes.

The sky stops its colour.
The storm from the East purges – whiteout
as though the Earth herself gulped those men down

gulag, gulag, gúlag, gulag, gulag.

In Tura they told us come spring
bones of fingers and toes
knuckle their way up like snowdrops.

I'm conspicuous but unwatched,
anonymous in this terrible landscape.
I've never slaved a day in my life, not like that,

not with such yearning, such muttered song,
so here are the meagre flowers,
the bend to one knee

precipitating the howl
toward speech, each petal
blazing.

The Second Before Disaster

Can you describe it?
The water before the stone's first ripple

Can you describe it?
The shuck that housed spring's late shoot

Can you describe it?
The lapse before the brain senses the hand is burnt

Can you describe it?
Waking to a sound I hadn't yet heard

Can you describe it?
The skin of an over-inflated balloon

Can you describe it?
A glass slips from my grasp

Can you describe it?
Heisenberg's principle doesn't allow it

Can you describe it?
Unutterable loss, present before the absence

Survey North of 60°

We're here to cast off names –
Viking, Fair Isle, Faeroes,
pronounce drowned coves, remap the coast.
I'm troubled – not at the cliff's seaward shiver
or the guillemots' black beaks scissored and shrieking –
but the wind singing
one long low note
its worm-burrow to the heart of the Arctic.

Late, in your hotel room,
we nip at a bottle of Absolut,
talk of tongues of ice:
Novaya Zemlya, Svalbard, Barents.
I don't mention the wind tunnelling me
like the wisteria that arched the path
from the park to my childhood home
where I'd sneak a smoke
to inhale the boy I thought I loved
before I knew what love was;

snow-quiet, mighty, obliterative,
to be able to sit at the world's end
and say little of it.

Pellestrina

We could make it here: two buses and a boat away from civilization
on this sickle of sand, this searing heaven,
all sky, sky and the tide blending, cerulean,
become zenithed, heightened.
I could survive on sun and sleep,
grow thin and strong, run clean
as long as you stand there – where my mind holds you
pointing out what I'd otherwise miss:
a crab shuttling for cover,
a cormorant's needle-dive into the swell,
the moon-round of a jellyfish,
its bell pulsating with light.

Riddle

I'm a beginning born from an end:
stars die bearing me.
My youth cries
fire, anvil, hammer.
I kill but can't be blamed.
Middle-aged, I'm the highest honour
of fallen empires –
for Russia they hung me by a red silk ribbon.
In the end though Wales is my lodestone,
those purpose-built towns
where Thatcher had it in for me –
my death the derivation of irony.

Abandoned Airfield at Dunkeswell

The height of summer. I thread my shadow
along the runway's vein of moss.
Nothing remains to mark the point
from which to look down
the length of sun-soft strip
that speeds back to this:
the hangar's simple machines of history,
the pop-rivet gun and punch clock,
the workbench morse-code of chisel and nail.

Pray for the fathers who took flight
that they lifted themselves away gently
but also for those housed in echoing halls
returning year after year
like swallows, to build.

Rose in Late Summer

All spring drought – but the rose has been patient
held herself courtly until the autumn rains
shake her into her own attentiveness.
Spiral ascending, corralled by sedge –
the secret knotted world of fox and rabbit.
She succumbs to the dark's ugly latching
to let the leaves start, then climbs thorn by thorn,
emerges whiter than the edge of dawn.

She gives of herself utterly
the way a sun-kissed house throws open its shutters,
each petal a loved, tremulous gasp
a small surrender to her inevitable task:
to waste herself joyously, but with care,
to fight clear then strip bare.

The Execution of Lady Jane Grey
(Paul De la Roche)

He ends it here.
Saves me from my own spectacle
with a white silk blindfold, has me counselled,
cosseted and fearful,
guided down to my knees,
muscles soft as butter, beseeching.

In truth I'm scaffolded on Tower Green,
snare beats bruiting *treason*, *treason*.

The crowd bays like my dogs circling a deer.
I hear my horses stamp in their stable, snort.
I tie my blindfold. I need no counsel.
I am a Queen.

Octopus Hunting

I settle to the shape of the trench and wait,
Elephantine in a nest of rock
One eye half open.

I flaunt camouflage, mimicry,
My eight arms poised
To claim the unworthy.

Evolution blessed me:
My supple mantle, my pinched beak,
My three hearts, none of which know mercy.

Now I'm Evolution's arbitrator.
I kill the curious, the weak,
I am death's artistry, spectral –

I drift through years of ocean.
My path the will of the tide,
Not quite chance, not quite calculation:

The weight of water propels me.
The volume of its darkness swells my cloak
to bursting, I know no satiety.

Postcard of a Break-Up Written at Edinburgh Castle

To tell you about the weather
I should first explain how the Sun –
sluggish with the weight of winter –
rolls back the haar.
To compare the city's slow reveal
to a bride lifting her veil,
although accurate,
misleads.

Dear John,
I'm sorry I didn't write a letter
but in short see reverse
for a picture of Mons Meg
the most powerful cannon ever built
which turned out to be a damp squib.

The Visitation

Night rolls out its road.
We speed along hedged by dark forest dark sea,
ink-coarse, formless but impenetrable,
dumbfounded the Moon slips away to recover herself
leaving our headlights the sole source of light,
zoetropes repeating a scope of bramble and fern
until a stag – caught mid-step on the bank –
a momentary megalith of antler and flank.

You didn't see him, held, hallucinatory
and the visitation over so quickly
I couldn't be sure, but I felt a poverty
as though some great knowledge passed me.
What'll become of us – the Moon's corollary –
hurtling, speechless.
How a sharp turn of the wheel
could save or discard us.

News

It's October in Newton-le-Willows.
In Exeter too it rains ceaselessly.
Sleep is lost on me but not this garden
where I sit constellate but apart,
not naming the stars but the dark.

I can't help but compare cancer
to an asteroid's silent accretion;
its slow bone-grind resolve into being,
how it whirls into our lives like a slungshot,
a fire-bolt, besieging.

But Sister its light is not yours.
Yours is not a flare or pulse, but long-light
unaffected by seasons, the come-and-go
of the universe's wider workings.
Your light is the beacon we signal
to navigate the night.

On Worthiness

But then explain the butterfly:
not its clubbed antennae
or dynamics of four-winged flight
but why it pinned itself to your chest
that day we waded through a field of wildflower –
every direction the siren yellow
of gorse and horseshoe vetch.

The Moon to the Sun Approaching Eclipse

Each night brings you closer; I wait, tethered
to the sea, reflect on my life ploughing
furrows in water, my litany of wrecks.
I'm an old penny – my body dull but its vow
still peaks wave-bright – like you, I long to be spent;
flare the way a match flares down to its heart
submit to the inevitable length
of our stately practiced arc.

Yet though you and I know the other lonely,
we'll only bring the Earth to a brief stop,
our pas de deux a dance of two solos
each half a gift of our oppositeness:

me a flitter of warmth and light, alive,
you spinning dumbly through the night.

Fugue

Midnight, the mind's sounding

the Moon an inverted pendulum
plumbing the sky's depth.

I crevice in your lee and wait;
for the charcoaled morning, its soft engine
of blue tit and goldfinch in blossom,
for the tree to loosen its heartwood clot –
a throb of bees
turning the dark slowly over like a thought.

I imagine their brothers
over-wintered, lumbering from sheds and rafters,
slow under February's papery Sun
but determined as rumour
clamouring to a hum
the hivesong's collapsed chorus –

to drop, to drop, to drop
like spring's first rain
onto the pale tongue of a flower.

Ghost Shark

Millions of years on
Megalodon swims its half ghost
through the ether of museum-space
part-shark part-reconstructed cartilage
top-jaw hoisted for a pig-eyed profile
made an example of.

But who's to say unequivocally
that at this exact moment she's not
holed-up in the wreck of an old war
nursing in the cold vault of our history
or charnel-mouthed over its huddled bodies
who's to say there's no glint in her dead eyes.

After all where better to see-out extinction
than from beyond the last glimmer of sunlight
where her movements sound like whispers
in our deep water soundings.
Who's to say she isn't just beyond our reach
Who's to say she shouldn't stay that way.

Dogger Bank

When the time's right
walk east from Wakering Stairs
along this mirror of waterlight
and gift the sea your grief –
for she thrives in such barren places,
making and remaking herself
until her blue breath heaves
and she comes up from under her own tide.

What's to be learnt
is at the mirror's edge, the lowest ebb,
where she meets her sister sea the sky,
water-bearer, drowner of absence –
that grief's flood is necessary to bring balance
and lead you back to dry land.

Notes

Early Sun: Gold has been associated with our star since ancient times. Every civilisation has a heavenly tale about the Earth's annual cycle of seasons, all of which focus on death in winter, the trial of darkness and eventual rebirth.

On Seeing Two Followers of Cadmus Devoured by a Dragon: The men in this painting were followers of the mythological Phoenician prince Cadmus who founded the city of Thebes, and from whom the element Cadmium gets its name.

Memorial at Norilsk: The gulag archipelago of Norilsk in Russia is home to Norilsk Nickel, a private mining company whose initial plant was built by those detained in camps between 1935 and 1956 as political prisoners against the State. It's still not known how many died in its construction.

The Second Before Disaster: Osmium tetroxide is rumoured to have been an ingredient in the bombs in the London bombings of 2005 and failed terrorist plots since. It is a catalyst, acting to speed up the reaction process. As such, if used in a bomb, there would be an infinitesimally small lapse between the catalyst working and the explosion.

Survey North of 60°: Yttrium is named after the small Swedish village of Ytterby, just south of the Arctic Circle. Multiple lines of evidence support very substantial Arctic warming since the mid-20th century. It's likely (>66% probability) that humans have contributed to this.

Pellestrina: Cobalt is used to produce the famous blue glass of the Venetian islands, of which Pellestrina is one. This island, unlike the Venetian mainland, remains relatively free of tourists and is home to a small community of fishermen and their families.

Riddle: Iron mining in the UK came largely to a halt in the late 1970s with the deconstruction of the mining industry under the Conservative Government led by Prime Minister Margaret Thatcher, nicknamed the 'Iron Lady'.

Abandoned Airfield at Dunkeswell: Titanium is used extensively in aircraft manufacture. Dunkeswell is a village in East Devon which is home to a largely derelict WW2 airfield.

Rose in Late Summer: Rhodium is named after the greek word for 'rose'. It's rather gentle sounding name is at odds with its properties. It is inert against corrosion and most aggressive acids. It's chemical 'stubbornness' is not unlike the rambling rose's insistence to flower, whatever the odds.

The Execution of Lady Jane Grey: 'Zinc white' is an oil paint containing the metal. The inclusion of Zinc made it possible to portray pure white tones in oils, such as Jane's nightgown central in De la Roche's painting. His staging is imagined. Jane was executed before a limited public on Tower Green.

Octopus Hunting: There are centuries-old tales of giant octopuses dragging ships into the deep. Octopuses, like many other marine animals, have copper in their blood. This helps them survive at depth, as it is a more efficient carrier of oxygen than the iron in haemoglobin.

Postcard of a Break-up Written at Edinburgh Castle: Mons Meg (1449) was one of the largest cannons ever made, but was relatively ineffective due to overheating, meaning it could only be fired a few times in battle. The Germans during WW1 determined that adding Molybdenum to the steel in cannons solved this problem. Cannons then became a central piece of war artillery.

The Visitation: The stag is a common heraldic symbol, including of the town of Dotternhausen in Germany, surrounded by deep forest and near where Tungsten was first found.

News: Palladium was named after Pallas, the goddess of truth and wisdom. Also sharing the root name is the asteroid 2-Pallas, one of the four largest asteroids ever discovered which appears as a dark mass through powerful telescopes. Early asteroids and planetesimals grew by attracting smaller asteroids and debris to them by their gravity. This is figuratively similar to how a tumor grows, which as it grows larger, grows faster.

On Worthiness: Iridium is named after the Latin for rainbow, 'iris', because of the varied colours of its salts. The word 'iridescent' is derived in part from 'iris'. Many insects, most notably butterflies, display iridescence.

The Moon to the Sun Approaching Eclipse: Silver has been associated with the Moon since ancient times. Before the astronomical explanation was known, eclipses were commonly seen as poor omens.

Fugue: Scientific studies with bees show that their bodies pick up heavy metals, including chromium, while foraging. It also appears at raised levels in their honey. These studies suggest that environmental contamination with heavy metals is ubiquitous and, like the use of neonicotinoids, potentially harmful to bees.

Ghost Shark: Megalodon is a prehistoric shark species and one of the largest predators who ever lived. It's fossilized teeth, for some unknown reason, act as a deposition site for Manganese, which helps to preserve them. Although theories abound (due to the differing ages of the Manganese covering the teeth) that megalodon still roam the ocean, all scientific evidence suggests they died out approx. 2.6 million years ago.

Dogger Bank: Dogger Bank is a large sandbank in a shallow area of the North Sea that forms the start of the famously deadly public path, the Broomway. The strange, mirroring reflections of Mercury are akin to the disorientating effect of light on the sand.